cf

A living thing seeks above all to discharge *its strength —life itself is* Will to Power; *self-preservation is only one of the indirect and most frequent* results *thereof.*

NIETZSCHE.

THE AGE
OF
CRISIS

A Study of World Problems

by

ARNOLD ROSIN

JOHNSON

LONDON

ARNOLD ROSIN © 1962

Library of Congress Catalog Card Number: 62-15685

First Published 1962

SET IN 12/13 POINT PLANTIN AND PRINTED AND MADE BY THE
COMMERCIAL ART COMPANY, FIVE OAKS PRESS, JERSEY, CHANNEL
ISLANDS FOR JOHNSON PUBLICATIONS LIMITED,
11/14 STANHOPE MEWS WEST, LONDON, S.W. 7

PREFACE

THE ROOT question for the world today is: will Communism be put down by force, or will it triumph? Will Communist China side with Russia, or will she seek her own destiny? And in the final, decisive struggle, where does Germany—that great question-mark —fit in?

Now that Russia possesses thermo-nuclear weapons, an effective long-range bomber force and guided missiles, it is no longer possible for the West to deter her from using her combined strength which, in total warfare, means nuclear annihilation of the enemy—nothing less than the extinction of Britain and victory over the West.

For Communism is reaching its goal. It no longer menaces, it is winning. To strengthen and unite possible allies, to weaken and divide actual and possible enemies, are the aims of the Soviet State. Russian forces stationed in Eastern Europe are there not only to defend Soviet Russia from western attack, but also because they are the indispendable iron frame that binds the Soviet camps in Eastern Europe together.

Russia's overwhelming power and threatening attitude may soon compel the West-European world to abandon its comedy of petty politics and unite against Communism. What lies in store when Communism passes beyond its aims—let alone achieves them—no one has troubled to inquire. A Faustian struggle with every weapon and every technic known to man will take place. Nations, peoples, cities may go under in an atomic age whose final, decisive war is for supremacy and nothing

[5]

less. Numbers, mass, weight are never an assurance of victory—witness the Russo-Japanese war. Attack can come, and at any time. And it is in the swiftness of attack, annihilation and total defeat, that lies the greatest chance of victory. Standing up to danger, readiness for great sacrifices—only these qualities can save a nation from going under.

Before it was Russia alone. Today it is both Russia and China that face the United States and Britain, with Germany, that rising colossus, still the undecided factor. Whether Russia will be able to hold her empire is uncertain. Ever since the 20th Congress of the Soviet Communist Party in February, 1956, Eastern Europe has been in a ferment, more or less suppressed—and with brutal force. It is the one language enslaved people know, and the only one that wins out in the end. Popular risings (Berlin, 1953, to the Polish mutiny and the Hungarian insurrection, 1956) confront the West with the same intolerable choice: either to turn its back on brave men and women who attack Russian tanks with hand-made bombs, or risk a third world war.

The grip of Communism is a grim, pitiless, no-quarter battle of the Will-to-Power for world domination. With brutal audacity Communism is riding to victory, and it would be absurd to suppose that it is going to die, to disappear, or simply to vanish overnight. Communism does not suffer to be halted merely because we disapprove. Nor is there any burying our heads in the sand or weeping bitterly. Only dreamers believe there is a peaceful way out.

The possibility of a Soviet attack, and the chances of its success, is the fate of the West-European world centring in the United States. Contending powers will terminate only in final victory. Nothing less is imaginable, and a compromise merely a sham. New York,

Chicago, Los Angeles reduced to rubble, dead, dark, empty of life; mass extermination, suicide, misery and destruction ending in slavery—all is possible, making the last hours of Hitler's Germany seem like child's play. The picture is frightful. We may hide from such a climax, or we may foresee it *and be the masters of the day*—but its possibility is there.

The Soviet aim is world domination by any means. The Soviet leaders have three immediate goals: first, the prevention of significant German rearmament (nuclear weapons in German hands); second, the withdrawal of United States forces in Europe; and third, the breakup of NATO.

Foreign policy based on force will end in disaster. Men, ships and even aircraft are now obsolete as instruments of attack and defense. Force deceives the West into thinking it is secure when it is not and leads inevitably to war.

The West no longer holds all the winning cards: controlling the means of production and having absolute military strength. It is faced with Russian science, the colossus China, the uncertainty of Germany and the *fait accompli* of the Arab world. Communist penetration is strong in Iraq, Syria, and North Africa. The Communists are out to win; the West to prevent a third world war. Time and history are on the Soviet side. Before long the Russians will surpass the West in every field. For the West, Soviet power and influence constitute the problem of the day. Tactics vary, but the strategic aim remains the same. Conflict between East and West is inevitable. The one is going to win; the other will be destroyed.

Today there is no halfway measure, no third way out. The masses will be sacrificed to the relentless course of world happening. Freedom, justice, and truth will bow to power, money, and race which, in our century of true Romanness, stand out as the supreme forces.

Yet the future is not without hope. The question is: have we the necessary political and military genius to ensure a final triumphant phase in our Civilization? Or will we sink before the massive challenge of Communism, fifteen-hundred million strong, alive and growing?

Arnold Rosin

Paris,
November, 1961.

CONTENTS

CHAPTER ONE

THE STRUGGLE FOR THE MASTERY OF THE WORLD

RUSSIA AND THE United States are fighting out a great political war in open preparation for the real one to come—whether in this decade or the next or not for another fifty years none can tell. Each is contending for supremacy, each resolved to make its destiny the Destiny of the entire world.

Russia's industrial output is tremendous, exceeded only by that of the United States. But unlike her great rival, Russia is not obliged to divert the greater proportion of her resources to the increasing demands of civilian consumption. Moreover it is very probable, militarily, that Russia could not conquer the United States. On the other hand, it is uncertain whether the United States could conquer Russia—let alone prevent her overrunning and colonizing the whole European continent, the Middle East, and the coastal areas of Africa.

But the achievements of the Russian industrial revolution have been bought at a fearful human, and heavy political, cost. The standard of life is very low. The growth of the urban population by more than 50 million people has resulted in terrible overcrowding. Just as Lenin suggested that barbarous methods would be needed to drive barbarism out of Russia, so the campaign against Stalin had been conducted in some ways by the political methods of Stalin, since his own lieutenants had inherited the task of leadership. Changes in Soviet society since Stalin's death have produced a public opinion which exerts a marginal but increasing influence. Even at the lowest level of the State machine, the executive organizations are acquiring a life independent of the Party, which is supposed to control them. However, one thing has *not* changed; the struggle for power in the Kremlin still has a decided Byzantine air—the removal of Beria had a true flavour about it.

If the Soviet economy were to move forward rapidly while the economy of the Western world was retarded by a slump, the attraction of the Soviet régime would make itself felt beyond the under-developed countries. But it would not exist along with a Byzantine political system. Nevertheless one fact is clear: the political and economic pace of change in the Soviet Union has *not* slackened.

In post-Stalinist Russia, history, as if taking revenge for a period of artificially enforced political inertia, has quickened its tempo—and the end is not in sight. The managerial reform has raised the issue of regional autarchy, encouraged centrifugal forces, and brought nearer the major question of tomorrow, raised forty years ago and then lost in the Stalinist system: that of the workers' participation in management. The urgent need for more food has compelled Khrushchev to sponsor the transfer of State property to collective farms.

Lenin[1] was a true Muscovite who had broken with the

---

[1] World revolution was the major premise of all that Lenin wrote and did. In Lenin, as in Marx, there were always two conflicting strains. Lenin was *always* a revolutionary who passionately believed in the liberation of the workers. But he was also—and above all—an *organizor*, and therefore not one of those who were prepared to carry liberty to its logical extremity in anarchism. It is important to remember that Marx denounced "alienation" of the human personality of the worker inherent in Capitalism, and treated Socialism as the essential condition of the liberation of labour.

Westernizing traditions of Peter the Great, and with the Western traditions of humanity and democracy. Stalin learned his ways from Lenin. He was not hampered by Lenin's ideas of abstract justice or Trotsky's doctrinal rigidities. Lenin left Stalin the makings of the Russia we know today: all Stalin had to do was to gain personal control of it. The rest is history.

Lenin's October Revolution, which suppressed democracy by taking the name of the proletariat in vain, led the Russians into incredible suffering, and laid the foundations of the most oppressive tyranny in modern history.

Russia is emerging in a new form from which one day great things may spring. The important change which began with Stalin's death is still in being. The dynamic forces of the new Russia are moving in a direction which nobody can predict and which a Khrushchev can only hope to keep pace with by the exercise of the most inspired opportunism which, let it be said once for all, is his strongest characteristic.

The theory of Russia's mission of world domination, her avowed intention of a supremacy that will lead the world and create *the* society of the future (now claimed to be in the process of fulfilment), is far from faltering. The hour of triumph, however, is still far off. The Russians do not expect their ultimate victory only from war, although to them it is a necessary part of it, but also from the disintegration of Capitalism. This fervent belief in the ultimate victory of Communism,[1] because it

---

[1] The growing idea of a universal mission of world revolution, has achieved for Russia what the misguided doctrine of racial destiny achieved for Hitler-led Germany. It has released the national Ego and its out-and-out will to domination and world conquest from any restraint and complexes which might oppose it. It has prevented also the setting in of a *malaise*, which occurred in Germany.

represents to the Russians not only an historical necessity but—as they see it—their rightful destiny as the fore-runners of those who would eventually rule the world—is visualized as *predestined fulfilment*.

The important changes which have taken place since 1953 show no sign of coming to an end. Nor are Stalin's heirs prompted to any Western ideals or democratic aspirations. Fully aware that the dead tyrant had been strong enough to postpone the inevitable revision of an obsolete system of government, they have sought to strengthen the Communist régime, not to weaken it. The dependence on slave labour, on police terror, and on clumsy censorship has proved a drawback not only economically, but also politically. A new generation of better educated men needed to carry out the technological revolution, symbolized by the sputnik, emphasizes Soviet Russia's fervent desire to succeed in the sharp struggle for power. Events have thus brought Russia abreast of the West—if not ahead of it—in the capacity for massive retaliation. Consequently she can act with less hesitation and fear in such dangerous places as the Middle East, and eventually make her bid for world conquest.

Red China is a *fait accompli*.[1] But what about South America, Africa, and Southern Asia? The Communist Parties of North Korea, North Vietnam, Burma, India, Indonesia, Malaya, as well as a number of Latin American parties, have already shown signs of following China's lead. Driven by promises of "equality" and "freedom", the yellow race may unite with the black to

---

[1] Stalin, a calculating master of power politics but also a prisoner of an outdated ideology, considered foreign Communist parties as mere tools of Soviet power, *not* as independent bodies capable of seizing power themselves. The Chinese revolution—Communism's biggest success since 1917—*was carried out against his specific advice.*

overthrow the white man. Murder, insurrection, and revolt will be the order of the day. Leaders, trained by the Communists, will set up a Party and spread Communism to the very doors of the democratic world.

Neither China nor Japan had had any contact with Marxist thought before World War I; for the most part they remained outside it. Actually, it was Western and not Eastern ideas on which both China and Japan had drawn heavily. The Bolshevik Revolution planted its seed in the Far East,[1] but at first—and not for a long time—without any real results. Japan, with her capitalism developed along definite Western lines of trust and monopoly, and her proletarian masses, seemed more than ripe for revolution, and offered the most promising field for Communist infiltration. It was on Japan, and not on China, that early Bolshevik hopes of revolution were centred: the miscalculation is betrayed in the whole subsequent history of Communism in China and Japan. Although Communism persisted in Japan,[2] it did not exercise any definite influence on Japanese affairs, nor have the active following among the workers and intellectuals that Communism had in France.

China has exceeded the expectations of the Kremlin, placing herself in the front rank of world politics as a politico-military unit of terrific possibilities. (China, not Japan, was the subject of the Stalin-Trotsky controversy.) Lenin, with a keen insight into the future (how *far* into the future we will never know), and his undeviating eye to political and military events, hailed

---

[1] The first Japanese translation of the Communist Manifesto appeared in 1905. In 1911, an anarchist-terrorist group was uncovered and its leaders executed for conspiracy to assassinate the emperor.

[2] A Party was brought to birth in 1922, to be dissolved; but it was re-organized in 1926, and continued through the 1930's.

the Chinese Revolution of 1912[1] and paid due tribute to its leader, Sun-Yat-Sen. In the revolutionary masses of the East, Lenin saw the future allies of proletarian Europe, although his dreams were more of Persia and India—countries which at that time had scarcely undergone any Communist influence.

China no longer looks back to her great heritage, but eagerly ahead to Communism. Today, Mao Tse-tung[2] is the recognized and unchallenged leader of a growing Communist China,[3] where the most successful party outside the Soviet Union has achieved a spectacular rise to power in defiance of Marxist doctrines. But—*China does not wish to become one of Moscow's satellites.* She wants to be independent. Her geographical situation alone, her desire to be subject and not merely object of world happening, makes this inevitable. Yet her destiny is linked with that of Russia, both *Asiatic* powers, both cut off from the West in a world of their own.

The present argument between Moscow and Peking is being conducted in strictly Leninist terms, and the point of drama is disagreement about the inevitability of war. As far back as the Twentieth Party Congress in 1956, the Russians decided that Lenin's belief that the only way to global Communism lay through violence and war was outdated. Although the Chinese appeared to accept this major revision at the time, nevertheless they have since very sharply questioned the lengths to which Khrushchev has gone to avoid the risk of war, and

[1] "Politics," said Lenin, "begin where the masses are, not where there are thousands, but where there are millions, that is where serious politics begin." *Selected Works*, VII (English translation).

[2] One of the destiny-men of our age, it was he who said: "One human being out of four is Chinese."

[3] China's population is the largest on earth. It is increasing at the rate of 12 to 15 million per year and will exceed 700 million by 1965.

they have never subscribed to Khrushchev's conviction *that nuclear war would spell disaster for Communism as well as for Capitalism.*

But there is no sign that the Chinese are actively contemplating war. In spite of the withdrawal of Russian technicians from China and Chinese students from Moscow, it seems impossible that China can stand alone without Russia for at least some years to come.

Despite Khrushchev's decision to establish ideological unity on his own terms and secure unquestioned leadership of the Socialist bloc, the Sino-Russian alliance is purely ideological between people very different from each other in temperament, outlook, and tradition.

Judging from Chinese sources, Mao Tse-tung's military doctrine, unchanged since it was formulated in the twenties and thirties, is not considered out of date. His formula is in many ways similar to that of the Soviets but differs in important aspects.[1] He agrees that any future war will be a large-scale war, a war of masses, but thinks it will be of incomparably longer duration than is the Soviet view. He differs on the importance of the surprise element and certain universal technical factors. For him purely military considerations must be subordinated to ideological and *political* considerations. He relegates military factors into the background, making them directly dependent upon ideological and political ones. He believes that the most important military factor is the *mobilization of the masses*, without which victory is impossible. And he is certain of the victory of the

---

[1] Soviet military doctrine recognizes five constantly valid factors contributing to the outcome of war, factors formulated by Stalin as the basic principles of Soviet strategy: stability behind the lines, political morale of the army and civilian population, number and quality of divisions, army equipment, and organizational capacities of commanders of all ranks.

Socialist camp in the event of war. He knows, however, that at the beginning of any war the imperialists will have technical superiority, including tactical superiority; but this was so in the war against Japan and the civil war; and in neither case did the enemy know how to use its superiority to achieve a *strategical victory*. And he fully agrees with Soviet experts that *Blitzkrieg* is out-dated and that future war, with atomic weapons, will last many years, even decades. But all Chinese tactics and stratagems rest on the assumption that such a war *will be waged on Chinese soil*, where the country's size will be utilized to advantage and thereby gain time for ultimate victory; for Mao Tse-tung and other Chinese leaders fully realize that they are not yet in a position to wage war successfully on foreign soil, especially against a fully equipped modern army.

But there is opposition to Mao Tse-tung's radical views of the political factor and the popular masses in the event of a new war. Many leaders know that a future war will be a war of brains (intellect), not of the masses, and that victory will come to that side which is better equipped technically, better mechanized and armed. China's principal deficiency is the disparity between the *quantity* and the *quality* of her production. An all-out atomic attack on a primitive, technically under-developed and undefended China would cause so many casualties that any further resistance will be impossible.

Yet the decisive factor in a war is not machines or weapons but *men*. During the initial period of a war, deficiencies in quality or quantity of armaments can be compensated by the enthusiasm of the masses and, con-sequently, by their industry. Moreover, the enemy may possess any amount of arms and yet—as in the war against Japan and the civil war—they may be taken from him and later used against him with telling effect.

Despite these views Mao Tse-tung's policy has continued unchanged. The Stalinist concept that surprise attack in modern war is of secondary importance has had no (or very little) effect on it. One thing is certain: there is no practical defense against nuclear missile attack; a nuclear war would annihilate whole countries and their populations, killing at least 500 to 600 million persons; a surprise attack would undoubtedly give the attacker a certain advantage *but would not prevent retaliation.*

After Stalin's death the Kremlin blundered and vacillated in Eastern Europe until Khrushchev finally discredited himself in the Polish and Hungarian revolutions. This period of confusion in Moscow enabled Communist China to take the lead in formulating Communist policies—the crises in Poland and Hungary marked *the first intervention of China in the political affairs of Europe.* But in contrast to China the Soviet Union clearly has the economic and military power to lead the Communist world and to take independent action on the world stage. Moreover, Russia today is governed by men who have grown up or have been born since the Revolutions and have made their careers in the Party or State bureaucracy. In China power still rests with those who followed Mao Tse-tung on the Long March and organized the victory of Communism after the end of the Pacific war. China resembles a land of fanatics keyed up to the passions and austerities of a militant faith, Russia a land of arrogantly successful business men. Although China is the most populous country in the world, a territory with a population at least two and a half times that of the Soviet Union, Russia is an immensely strong power, many times stronger than China industrially and militarily. But the serious weakness at the top is due primarily to the exhaustion of the original *revolutionary impulse*.

Communist China is today the biggest and most problem-creating country in the world. Sooner or later the Communists who exercise effective authority over the whole Chinese mainland must oust Chiang Kai-shek's representatives as occupants of the Chinese seat at the United Nations. Britain has long since recognized Communist China but is now awaiting America's good pleasure before drawing the logical conclusion and lining up with the majority of neutral Asian and African countries favouring China's admission to the United Nations.

The Moscow-Peking quarrel is an ideological one about war and peace but in essence it is a quarrel about who should lead the Communist world. The Chinese leaders seem to be less conscious of the perils of nuclear warfare than the Russians, or at any rate less frightened by them. As a result the Moscow Communists have been forced to define their position with greater clarity and, under pressure from Peking, have begun to think about fundamentals in a way undreamt of since the death of Lenin.

Yet Khrushchev's manoeuvres and policies stem directly from an elaborately thought out master plan for the subjugation of the world *including China*. He still relies on what Stalin used to call the proper basis of international policy, *the calculation of forces*. But for a long time the Chinese have been publicly criticizing Soviet policies or tactics. It is no surprise therefore that Khrushchev has been making a spirited and calculated bid to regain for Moscow the moral leadership of the Communist bloc, which for some time has been in abeyance. Yet if the Russians believe that a major war can be avoided, the Chinese continue to insist that war is inevitable because that is the only way to end imperialism—and the sooner imperialism is crushed the better. Mao Tse-tung has stated that even if 200 million Chinese were killed in a nuclear war more than enough would survive to build a Communist world. On June 1st 1960 Lu Ting-yi, Vice-Premier and Politburo member in charge of propaganda and culture, told a Peking congress that hopes for a live-and-let-live policy with the West "do not exist and never will exist." Two days later Liu Shao-chi, Chairman of the Republic, called for persistent struggles against the United States "to isolate it to the greatest possible extent." *Red Flag*, the Party's theoretical journal, has argued for months that after a nuclear war Communism would build a loftier civilization "on the brink of a dead imperialism."

One thing is certain: the Communist bloc, which used to have one head, now has two. But it would be dangerous folly to exaggerate the Sino-Soviet differences. The two giant Communist countries have far too much in common, especially the hostility between the West and their own civilization, to fall apart in the face of what they both regard as the common capitalist enemy. China still needs sustained Soviet aid for her industry, and depends on Soviet military support not only for aircraft and tanks, but even for the fuel-oil to run them. As for the Soviet Union, the collapse of a Communist régime along her eastern frontier would be sheer suicide.

The issue is more than of personalities. The Soviet Union has a large and not yet fully digested empire, a highly industrialized economy and parity with the United States as a leading nation. China, on the other hand, has a large irredentist cause in Formosa and the off-shore islands, a stored-up Asian resentment against Western "imperialists," and a grievance from being barred from the United Nations. But precisely because her territory is under-developed and overpopulated, she has a better chance than any other world Power of surviving a third world war. The Chinese leaders are sincerely convinced of the weakness of the "imperialist bloc" and the invincibility of the Socialist. Their own history supports this belief: they succeeded in conquering China at a time when the Kuomintang possessed far superior forces.

Mao Tse-tung has always stood for the independence of the Chinese Party and State.[1] Already at the end of the 1920's he opposed not only Moscow but also the Comintern. His efforts to build up a peasant army and unleash a civil war ran counter to Stalin's plan. Stalin was attempting to create a classical Communist Party in China made up of the working class. In 1935 Mao liquidated the Party leaders sent from Moscow. At the end of 1936 he contradicted Moscow again when he defended the theory of "national paths to Communism," protesting against the Soviet theory that *every Communist State must tread the path of the Soviet Union.*

The 1961 leadership of Communist China is, with few exceptions, identical with that of 1951. In contrast to Soviet turnover, there is a cohesive élite with a self-conscious ideological discipline. The Chinese Communist challenge to Western interests in Asia is both real and dangerous. The People's Republic of China, established by Mao Tse-tung in October 1949, is an avowed

---

[1] Stalin had a tendency to ignore the independent and equal position of the Communist parties and Socialist countries in the international union. Mao did not compromise with Moscow and recognize the leading role of the Soviets until as late as November 1957, on the occasion of the fortieth anniversary of the October Revolution, but then—judging by reports from Belgrade—only after long arguments.

Communist régime with its main enemy defined as "world capitalism led by American imperialism." Soviet technical assistance and training for China's atomic research program makes it reasonable to expect the first Chinese nuclear test explosion in less than two years. The West has fought two wars with Asia within the past two decades. The next one may be the last.

Japan is today an incalculable country, with power to affect the course of world events.[1] Not only does it present a fertile soil for Communism, but emotionally it is singularly explosive.[2] The prime interest of the West in Japan is not simply that it should be able to use its territories for bases. *It is to prevent Japan from going Communist.* Without bases in Japan America might be unable to defend South Korea. But from Okinawa, and from much further south, from the Philippines, the United States can mount a deterrent against any expansionist move by Chinese forces, whether against Formosa, or in the Seato area, or even against India. Distances in the Pacific are enormous, and in future war, especially one fought with conventional weapons, the more bases the better. But the focus for the protection of South and South-East Asia is really the Philippines.

An alliance between Powers of unequal strength is tolerable only when the weaker country solicits protection, openly or privately, not when protection is forced upon it. Japan is no exception.

Communism in Japan would give the Communist

[1] Japan, by her wars, has played a fateful part in history. The Russo-Japanese war was to undermine the Tsars; the Sino-Japanese war of 1894-95 prepared the fall of the Manchu dynasty; her war which began in 1937 was to complete the Communist revolution.

[2] The Tokio riots and the frustration of Eisenhower's visit were the first fruits of Russia's test of the chances of breaking America's alliances in Asia.

[23]

cause throughout Asia a very alarming fortification. The danger is that a frustrated instinct towards pacifism may be taken hold of by Communist countries and exploited for bringing in a Government which, though non-Communist, would not merely be unco-operative with the West but also be the rallying point of all the anti-American forces in the Far East, reviving old, disturbing ambitions frustrated in the last war.

For Russia it is not the person, not the soldier, the factory worker or the peasant that matters, but the *Idea* of Communism, and it is for the sake of the *Idea* that millions have died and millions more will march, eagerly, to their death. With Communism the future for Russia is set. All that matters is not political passions, not even Party interests, but that the institution survive. The individual—worker, peasant, soldier, artist—bows to the greatness of the State.[1] Again, it is the *Idea* of the State that has finally mastered: the priest is conspicuously absent. From Leningrad to Odessa, from west to east, there is only one kind of pulse, one kind of moral, taste, manners, customs, and thought. Public opinion is formed everywhere by *men*, not books. "People's rights" simply do not exist.

---

[1] Whereas Russia attempted to abolish the clergy, the nobility, and the bourgeoisie as classes, the Bolshevik class system of workers, peasants, soldiers underwent many changes before a final constitution was adopted in 1936. Today, long after Stalin's death, the system is still undergoing changes. Yet theoretically there are no classes in Russia. There are high officials in the Communist Party and Government; intellectuals, artists and writers; minor officials numbering millions of engineers, technicians, statisticians, economists, teachers, police; industrial workers of all types, crafts and skills—plus the military and forced labour (criminals, prisoners of war, etc.). In short, the society in Russia today is that of a totalitarian State rapidly assuming a blatant class-structure so utterly at variance with everything those long-dead fighters for freedom and equality ever dreamt of.

Russia has won her victory,[1] and this no one can deny. From a decaying, corrupt aristocracy has come to life, in an unbelievably short time, one of the great Powers which, together with Red China, is out to conquer the world. The spirit of the army is, as before, a political power on its own accord, including of course the Navy and the Air Force, and it becomes a serious question how far the State is master and how far tool of its army.

Russia's true history lies in the future; the slumbering Russian world-feeling still awaits its unfolding—and that will manifest itself in the birth of a new religion. For us—let there be no mistake about it—the age of theory is at an end. That of Marx has had no successor, China and Russia must, and *will*, cling together for an indefinite period. Yet each is a separate country with separate destinies. China's change to Communism is a revealing sign that *the tide of Western power is turning*. Communism has never ignored the underlying *human* element that makes up State and world politics. Nor has it ever underestimated the extent to which the execution of any policy depends on the enthusiasm and the initiative of the individual citizen, whether he fights in battle or stands before a machine. One thing is certain: he who controls the army leads the people. The Will-to-Power is stronger than any theory. Moreover, China is dependent on Russia for her industrial development, for her modern army and air force, and for most of the petrol and other essentials of war. *That* is her position in the fight for power and world domination, the position of a steadily increasing, fateful rift between

[1] When Russia emerged from World War I as the first Marxist state, many of the ablest political observers in Europe and the United States were convinced that it could not survive. As late as 1926 many were still predicting that it would collapse within five years or less.

two giants—the one soon strong enough to raise his hand against the other.

Soviet Russia believes that an attack from the West is her inevitable fate. To "liberate" new areas of Europe, to seek control of the East, is nothing more than a practical politico-military plan to achieve the greatest possible defense against a coming Western attack. Besides, Russia is not compelled, as was Hitler's Germany, to attain her aims quickly, within the lifetime of her present hierarchy. She can afford to wait years until the expected decay of the West and the follies of its leaders and rulers impel the West-European world to a suicidal attack.

The advance of Soviet armies into Eastern and Central Europe in 1945 as a very important part of the final phase of the struggle against Hitler brought Moscow's political and military authority to the very centre of Europe, representing a major alteration in the world strategic political balance. But armed forces today differ greatly from those of 1945; the theory of waging successful war has advanced far ahead. Long-range missiles, with their effective mass destruction,[1] provide considerable opposition for delivering a surprising blow, whose intensity and strength outstrip anything known to date in the history of warfare. The key to the arms race is the question of *invulnerability*. Not the size of nuclear weapons but the ability to deliver them effectively. How to penetrate the opponent's defenses and keep rockets and bombers safe from attack. Yet new weapons, however powerful they may be, cannot by themselves determine the course and outcome of a war and do not reduce the decisive import-

---

[1] Einstein has estimated that in the next war two-thirds of the populations involved will be killed. And this is a conservative figure.

ance of ground, air, and naval forces.[1] Realizing the enormous destructive power of modern weapons, the Soviet leaders are attempting to make Russia's economy and hinterland as invulnerable as possible as opposed to New York, Chicago, Los Angeles, which are highly populated, industrial cities.

Khrushchev has adapted the concept of world revolution to the changed conditions of today.[2] For Stalin, warfare by means of regular armies was the only possible means of promoting world revolution. In contrast to Lenin and some of the Bolsheviks, he did not rate highly the chances that the Communist movements in individual countries might launch a revolution on their own or the ability of the Comintern to organize and lead such revolutions. But like Lenin, he was convinced of the inevitability of profound conflicts between the "imperialist" States which must lead to war. Until his death, Stalin remained convinced that the essential tool for affecting world revolution on the basis of an international war was not the armed proletariat but *a regular army*.

The development of weapons of mass destruction made it obvious to Stalin's successors while Stalin was alive that this view was obsolete. The first hydrogen

[1] Motke's views that strategic errors committed at the beginning of a war cannot be retrieved are obsolete. Soviet military theories stress that one all-out strategic move will not be enough in a modern war; there must be *several* such moves.

[2] Lenin foresaw the victory of Communism in other countries as a result of a proletarian revolution organized from within or inspired from without; Stalin as a result of Soviet military aggression, which would give power to local Communists by the staging of "popular democratic" elections. Khruschev has now supplemented this strategy with a new type of revolution. Henceforth victory will be possible also by a third method: Soviet economic aggression. But this new economic doctrine of achieving world domination by no means excludes the Leninist formula of direct action: revolution and war.

[27]

bomb signed the death warrant of large-scale warfare and made classical means of warfare valid for the promotion of world revolution. For Khrushchev the Soviet Army is no more than a means of intimidating the West and exerting a constant pressure upon the non-Communist world. As an instrument of *direct* action, it has largely lost its value.

An invasion of Western Europe and the thrusting back of Russia is possible only after great destruction, incredible misery, and huge loss of life. But the consequences would be disastrous with the possible disappearance of our civilization. *And yet this is what we are heading for.* Now that the Russians have turned their backs to Stalinist assumption that the Soviet Army[1] is the only vehicle of Communist expansion (an empty assumption in an age of nuclear deterrents), the Western countries will be faced with a greater challenge than the armoured divisions on the Elbe.

Once Russia was a problem for Asia. Now she is a problem for Europe and America. Before, Russia was an impending threat. Now that threat has become a certainty. Since 1900 Russia's population has increased by half, despite wars, famines, and revolutions, and there is no reason to believe that it will not double itself by the end of the century. For, like China, there is no space problem. The vast and relatively undeveloped hinterland[2] provides ample room for expansion and for

---

[1] In 1946, with the Western armies being demobilized and the Americans withdrawing to their distant continent, Europe lay open to the Red Army which had retained and developed its strength; had it moved it would have been checked only by the use of the atomic bomb.

[2] Khruschev himself has stated that the enormous areas available in the Soviet Union make possible the decentralization of industry, thus preventing its total destruction in war.

tremendous growth in the decades to come. Moreover, Russia has undergone tremendous changes. Think of the difference between Napoleon's Russia (1812) and Tolstoy's (1910), between Lenin's and Stalin's,[1] and of the gulf that separates Tsarism from Communism. Russia, which Peter the Great annexed to Europe, is once again part of Asia, *to which she has always belonged.*

Russia fought World War II as a *total* war, the United States found it relatively harmless. The American people experienced no house-to-house defense, no scorched-earth policy, no terrifying all-out night-and-day attack, no taking of hostages, no mass executions. Russia drove back the Nazi hordes at the tremendous cost of lives and destruction. Countless defenders of the State —witness the battle of Leningrad—were slaughtered defending their land, their city, their very homes against the enemy.[2] Fighting on foreign soil, the United States won the war by mass superiority, by technical perfection in ground, aerial, and naval warfare.

History is moving towards a great decision. A new world has arisen, a world that has conquered a third of the globe, and is out to conquer the rest. No one dares to recognize or seriously consider the *relentlessness* of its advance, which is moving unchecked to its ultimate destiny. Whether fulfilment or defeat, our age will decide. And this decision is near at hand.

Peter the Great hailed a period of European penetration of Russia, making the Muscovite world a paradise

---

[1] Stalin lived too long. What would have been Russia's fate if Lenin had lived ten or even twenty years longer? The Russian Revolution would have certainly taken a different turn, avoiding the inevitable struggle for dominance—Trotsky exiled and later murdered, Stalin emerging as dictator and supreme ruler.

[2] In 1945, the Soviet Union counted 30 million dead, including the flower of Soviet manhood.

for foreigners and heretics, but not without turning Russia into one of the great European powers. Stalin inauguarted an epoch of Russian penetration of Europe and Asia, and perhaps—no one as yet can foresee to what extent—of the whole world.[1]

The Russian is Asiatic, not Western. He lives in a closed-in world kept down by force of arms, and he knows no other. He reads *Pravda* and believes what he is told. As a disciplined religion, Soviet Communism has long since hardened its cohorts to accept cataclysm as a necessary part of the "normal" process towards world power and eventual world domination. Communism sees no compromise between endless struggle for survival and a promise of ultimate salvation. The West does.

[1] The parallel is worth observing in Philip IV's (Lenin, Stalin and their successors) idea of world monarchy and world domination (Communism) in Habsburg hands (Russian), with the centre of world politics in Madrid (Moscow), and with an eye to India and America—the Empire-idea (The Far East, China, Europe, and eventually both North and South America).

CHAPTER TWO

GERMANY, THE GREAT QUESTION-MARK

G ERMANY IS the *key* country of Europe, if not of the whole world. This age-old nation of warriors is again that of men fit for arms, calling for spiritual self-preservation, honour, and self-respect. Germany's eternal, forceful way of life has elevated the nation to the highest intensities, a living and battling nation possessing not only a condition of movement but also (and above all) an *Idea* to which everything is sacrificed.

Germany stands historically and strategically between the United States and Russia. Germany is divided and aspires to unity. She has lost her provinces and wants them back. She was beaten decisively and many Germans want to efface the defeat. The unsatisfied longing for a united Germany, the expression of the feeling of *expanse*, the will-to-history—all is there.

The life-power of Germany understands not nobility or elegance or even ideas but *reality*. And the major part of the decisions of world history is contained in *esprit* of this kind. Germany's unrestrained passion for fighting, risking, thrusting forward is nothing less than the passion for destiny. It is precisely why the nation understands little of quiet, happiness, or enjoyment. Germany is the real *force* of Europe, dangerous, powerful, unpredictable, ready to prove that History is free of laws but heavy with fate.[1] If politics is war by other "peaceful" means—the art of the possible—then Germany is already the victor.

Because of her geographic position and her formidable economic development, Germany is today in the centre of the struggle for power. To defend Germany from Communism and to arm her against Russia—this is the problem of the Western Powers, but it concerns Germany as well. If long-term defense of the West is to be assured, Germany *must* be rearmed. *But the risks are great.* To create an army is one thing, to ensure that it will fight, and fight effectively, is something else. There is nothing more stupid than the hope of building up and rearming Germany in order to destroy Russia.[2] The danger is realized in Europe. In the United States it is still not realized. For Germany's life-expression is struggle, and nothing but struggle, and it is the desire to win through to victory (whether in war or in peace), which decides whether its fate is to suffer the history of others or to be itself their history. The conflict is identical with Life itself. What matters is not how the nation achieves victory, *but where other nations stand*; not the *means*, but the *result*. Germany's greatness or inferiority depends on the depth or shallowness of its race-instinct

---

[1] *History is Destiny*, unfolded through the birth and death of cultured societies, developing from its vigorous form of creative spontaneity and religious devotion to the petrified stage known as "Civilization". Ours is not an age of Culture but that of Civilization. Culture has been put into books and reduced to museums. The facts of history as distinct from those of natural science are forever *men*, or *groups of men*, and the circumstances and events which they brought about.

[2] The Capitalistic countries hoped that the German and Soviet armies would mutually exterminate each other so that *neither* would again become a decisive factor in European affairs.

which boldly forgets the past in its eager desire to triumph in a future which it *dares* to envisage.

To Germany belongs the future—every nation has the right to call the future its own. Germany has provoked four major wars since 1866,[1] and the continuing vitality of the German people testifies to their age-old will to be masters, not slaves, and above all to be *free*.

Rearmed, Germany might attempt a liberation of the eastern part of the country in an effort to conquer her lost provinces. Or she might combine industrial and military might to accomplish her aim through diplomacy. Meanwhile Germany goes forward at a tempo that is both admirable and alarming. What she has accomplished in the last decade is unbelievable. What she will be in another decade is impossible to say. But so long as the country is divided not one German will find peace.

The Kruschev-instigated Berlin crisis emphasizes the importance of settling the outstanding problems of Germany's existence. The strength of the Western position over Berlin lies in its relationship to the tacit convention on which the peace of the world has depended since 1945. The Germans may grow disillusioned with Britain, France, and the United States but not with Germany which for them is the West. However their disillusionment with NATO they would prefer it to be subordinated to Russia.

The struggle between East and West offers no third solution to the German people. Mastery of themselves and readiness for inward sacrifice have long been their historical fate. The destiny of Germany is pursuing its course and *must* accomplish itself. The Will-to-Power—

---

[1] The "Seven Weeks' War" with Austria, Saxony, and Hanover, Prussia's victory over Austria and the Peace of Prague.

the most genuine of all race-feeling—presupposes recognition of the adversary, but not fear.

History knows no rules, no laws, only the *success* which makes one nation master and others slaves. Germany has a goal to achieve, a mission to fulfil, a will to carry out. Germany is not a static nation; she wants her logical destiny in world politics. And it is to the East that Germany looks to satisfy her ambitions. Rearmed and led by experienced generals and officers who still look to the sword for glory, honour, and tradition. Germany will soon be powerful and dangerous enough to dictate her terms to both the West and the East. And once on top she will have the trump card to play against all odds.

The Soviet plan for the Communization of the world envisages the annexation not of countries which have been devastated by a full-scale atomic war, but of flourishing States, whose populations and resources can be exploited either by successive minor wars or by *coups d'état* carried out with the aid of the Soviet Army. These basis theses of Communist theory which state that it is the Soviet Union's task to support the "oppressed peoples" of other countries were formulated by Lenin and Stalin[1] and, in spite of revision, have remained unaltered.

The wresting of Germany from the non-Communist camp and her inclusion in the Communist empire would bring the date of the final attack on the non-Communist world much nearer. Moscow has planned the practical implementation of this policy in two stages—first, the neutralization of Germany and her withdrawal from NATO and secondly, the spreading of Communism, both politically and socially, throughout Germany, with the

---

[1] Stalin, *Problems of Leninism*, 1947, 4th ed., p. 102.

aim of subordinating her economic potential to the demands of Soviet policy and extending the borders of the Soviet empire to the Rhine and beyond, practically to the Atlantic ocean.

Just as the seizure of Czechoslovakia by Germany in 1938 left Hitler free to deal with Poland, so too the conversion of West Berlin into a free city might well open the way for Soviet pressure on West Germany and then on all the NATO countries.

The force of Communist attack cannot be weakened by pacts, theories, or disagreements between the non-Communist world and the Communists but only by an actual growth in the defensive power of the non-Communist world and its firm decision to use force when necessary for the elimination of Communist aggression.

The destiny of the West will be determined not by frontal attack across Europe but by *encirclement,* with the vital left wing of the pincer movement proceeding between the Persian Gulf and the Atlantic coast of Morocco. "Preventative action"—the theorist's favourite catchword—is made impossible by atomic strategy. Keen military minds, however, know that they must rely on men rather than on technics and reckon fighting spirit, battle training, and strategical flexibility more important than fire-power in terms of kilotons of explosive. The NATO Powers have found no way of holding the western fort and, at the same time, protecting the important southern flank of the West.

Nothing short of European federation can yield a comprehensive and *effective* defense system. For only the age-old spirit of national pride and patriotism can make good fighting men.[1] The proud blood of the

---

[1] Not college boys trained in ninety days to meet a sudden need and swell the office-corps. Uniforms do not, and never did, make soldiers, let alone men.

beast of prey revolts against war-tactics reduced to making the machine do the fighting work of man. The proud Russian soldier has proved to fight the better for being uncomfortable and above all for defending his native soil against aggression. *There is no substitute for military genius.* Just as history is written by men who make their destiny in a world of strong living, so wars are won by those with a boldness and determination to prove that, though Nature is the stronger of the two, man's privilege is the Viking-tradition of fighting to victory.

Nineteenth-century Prussianism, which can be suppressed but not wiped out, has left a permanent mark on the German people. The Prussian spirit, that standard of military leadership which ruled supreme from Frederick the Great to Moltke and created immortal fame for Hitler's generals[1]—still lives on, alive and growing. It showed itself effective in 1870, 1914 and again during the entire phase of World War II. Meanwhile Americans rejoice at the thought of "European Unity," while the very possibility that a Europe under German control might make a successful "deal" with Russia, is not even considered. History has sprung great surprises in the past. She can do so, again, in the future.

If Germany turns to the West the whole context of the Western powers—military, political, economic—will at once be superior to that of Soviet Russia and her

---

[1] The greatest of whom was Von Rundstedt. Not only was he the ablest German commander of World War II, but he also represented the epitome of the Prussian military spirit and its undeviating tradition. He stood for that unthinking devotion to duty and obedience to command, which is nothing more than the substitute for German civic consciousness. Like a true Prussian, he served to the end, knowing that the war was lost and victory impossible, that the Fuehrer was half-insane, and that useless prolongation of fighting meant only greater disaster.

satellites. But if Germany goes over to the East (which is more than a possibility), the balance of military, political, and economic power would tend towards equality. Then with the aid of Germany, Soviet Russia would have an easier task of holding together her new empire in Europe and a better chance of controlling Communist China—and in time might find the strength to risk an all-out war against the West.

Nothing can stop Germany, not even Russia, let alone the United States. Enriched by experience, hardened by suffering and disaster, Germany is no longer object, but subject, of history. Whether she will side with the West against Communism, or throw in her lot with Russia—or step aside to allow East and West to fight it out *and then emerge victorious*—no one can yet predict. One fact is certain: Germany's imperialist tradition may still be strong enough to subdue the masses to the workings of vast historical processes.

CHAPTER THREE

MONEY AS FORCE AND POWER

WITH THE DEATH of Napoleon ended the era of the military hero. Instead, a new power came into being to shove aside the world conqueror, and to end once and for all dreams of glory with sword and cannon. *Its name was money.* Politics took a new direction, a totally different shape and form. Without money there would be no prosperity, no political and economic leadership, no peace and war.

The Industrial Revolution began in 1760, the year the flying-shuttle appeared. England quickly began to dominate the economic world. Her fleet, second to none, served the economic interests of the country. Had the British government decided to throw in its lot with the Confederate South, the whole course of the Civil War would have been altered. The North defeated, the money power and might of the United States would have been centred elsewhere. Instead of Boston, Pittsburg, and Chicago giant cities like Richmond, Charleston, and Savannah would have arisen to write a new and different chapter in the history of the United States and —eventually—of the whole world.

This all belongs to the past. Today it is the dollar bill, the British pound, the German mark that determine the politico-economic destiny of the Western world. Backed by gold they represent the power that is synonymous with their denomination, increasing and declining as the market rises and falls—all reflecting world events.

For today money is an *integral* part of civilized life. The greater the wealth concentrated in the hands of individuals, the more the fight for political power develops into a question of money. This, and nothing else, is the meaning of the word "Money" for us. Governments come and go, revolutions break out, armies are slaughtered; but money as an *idea*, as a force and power that more than once have made history—lives on.

That which stands in the centre of our civilization, completely dominating the formulation of ideas, is the industry of machines with its world trade and export industry without which England could not exist. In such a setting, encompassing the entire earth, money becomes dominant and its activity second to none. It sides with political, parliamentary, revolutionary power. It prevails over all other forms of force—the chosen vehicle of energy, more powerful, more destructive, more meaningful, than has ever before been imagined. It brings certain men to power—destiny-men of our time—bold, energetic, audacious, who see Capitalism or Socialism only in terms of moneyed force and power. The basis of all political reality is nothing less than the *triumph of money*.

This overlordship of money and intellect is the key to the struggle for the mastery of the world, while the masses—formless by definition—look on in bewilderment, apathy, or resignation—and, as always, ready to accept without question the fate that will be imposed on them. For, in reality, every nation is represented in history by a *minority*. It is distinctive of the *élite* idea that is capable of leading a nation to victory and of giving its own being a greater sense of superiority. Men are *not* equal. Montaigne knew this, so did Shakespeare. Society is made up of those who live in the grand sense of the word and those who merely exist, those who lead and those who are led, those who reap vast profits and those, millions, who slave away without leaving a trace.

Money is a *force*. Its *effect* is what matters. Money is born in the mind, and it is the one idea that defies Time and Space. It is past, present, and future simultaneously as parts of each other. Money defies mitigating circumstances, dismisses cherished hopes and illusory imagination. It buys men, armies, whole countries. The last and final expression of our civilization, it is Destiny itself.

For it is for money, and nothing else, that men live and fight and die, win through or fail. For millions it is the test of strength before which such time-honoured things as tradition, form, training, custom, intellect, are swept brutally aside. Money has no tag that gives away its source. Everywhere it is the essence of life, the very meaning of existence. Bigger profits are the sign of prosperity and success and, once tasted and enjoyed, can never be accepted for less. Saturated with the idea of money, this materialistic point of view not only dominates the entire thought and feeling of the West European world, it characterizes our age as well.

A new and significant chapter in world happening is taking place in the relationship between economics and politics; for whereas economics was the master of politics (England), politics is becoming the master of economics —witness the United States. Now, both of these make claims upon the life-feeling of the individual, and the confusion of our ideas is that the one is not separated clearly from the other.

Business success is one thing, political power another. To think in terms of politics means *to choose*. Money is *trade*, thinking abstractly of buying and selling, of profit and loss, of value and price, of success and failure. The politician directs the destiny of the State, the business man for whom money is a god, a religion, a complete way of life, turns his back to the other. *For him money is life.* He is interested in *his* profits, reckons according to *his* wants, and forces *his* offers upon others, raking in immense profits.

Money awakens the ugly, vulgar, greedy side of life, for the sake of which everything else miserably collapses, and the naked struggle for existence comes into its own. There is no contrast so profound as that between wealth as traditional culture and overnight riches. For the one money is second-nature, for the other it is synonymous with gaudy display. It is at bottom the double sense of big-city life, the opposition of a fine tradition that spreads and a get-rich-quick idea that forms itself pyramidally. As in ancient Rome, so in present-day United States the more extensive and populous the people, the more diversified the conditions and pursuits of its population—already more than 180 million—and the richer (money-powered), more luxurious and dissimilar the people, the more difficult it is to equalize the actions of the government. And naturally, the more easy for one portion or party to pervert its powers to oppress, rule, and plunder the other. Money, the servant of politics—as men like Talleyrand understood it and employed it successfully—becomes the master of man and the maker of history.

From landed to manufacturing interests, property is the true basis of power, forming separate interest in society. Out of the conflict of classes arises political discord and revolution. The idea is not new. It is as old as political science itself. For it has always been the struggle of classes—the one *despising*, the other *envying*—that has shaken so many nations to their foundations. The English Revolution of 1688 was a revolution in the form of property, as well as of other rights, which

[41]

men fought not to destroy, but to protect. And in every revolutionary upheaval, from which leaders arise, money takes a different shape and course. Consider the France of 1789, of 1812 and of 1848.[1] The bourgeoisie were neither nobles nor peasants, still less priests. They made up the city or town dwellers. Their power was derived not from birth or from office but solely and supremely from *money*, which, in turn, became an abstract and convenient measure of the material value of all things. With an eye to calculable cash, they were occupied with affairs touching the immediately practical. Time and Space for them were the clock and the ruler. Nor have they changed to this day, nor does it matter whether they are called "bourgeoisie" or "middle class"; the precise and indispensable symbol, that everyday sign of their activity, is *number*, which becomes the extension of all things (Space), and the meaning of all events (Time).

In the United States the business man and the general replace the skilled politician; rank and statesmanship give way to money and the narrowness of party-horizons.[2] But ex-bankers and powerful financiers are no match for strong race-quality, dignified life and a broad political outlook requiring a tactical superiority and an effective

[1] The profundity of a revolution is measured by the degree of *popular* activity. The English, French, and Russian revolutions were profound *mass social* revolutions as distinct from *political* revolutions. Civil wars occurred with newly created mass armies riding to victory proving how deeply into the masses the revolutionary spirit had penetrated. The European revolutions of 1848 were purely political movements. In France the sweep of the revolution did not parallel the storm of sixty years earlier.

[2] John Foster Dulles' European policy of the promotion of an American-German alliance—which the Germans eagerly thought would result in reunification and the rise of a new Germany with promise of grandeur—has not achieved even the beginning of reunification but the continued hard division of Germany and Berlin.

State-idea to see a nation through to victory. Money, again, is a *force*, not a practical political theory. Theories, like principles, move the masses only when money is concerned, because it is the only thing the masses really take seriously.

Today, big-city thinking is money-getting by means of money. Before the power of financial speculation, everything must give way—*this is the secret of Western economy*. For this money becomes sovereign. It is the one language common to all men in relation to activity rather than to flat formulas. Money is the opposite of the almightiness of God, and against it metaphysics and mysticism are useless. It is the difference between men who force money upon others and those who are maintained by money. This dominance of the moneyed class, with its emphasis on physical energy and economic determinism, coupled with fear and greed, shoves aside completely and unmistakably all possibility of religion and faith. Churches, chapels, synagogues exist only in relation to money and social morale: priestly direction and rabbinic approach have nothing whatever to do with capitalistic finance.

No one is wholly free of money. *But it is politics that rules*. It declares war and peace, decides the economic pattern of today and tomorrow, and in the battle of law and money it alone is victor. Economics is the basis of politics—but no more. Politics overrides continents, cities, peoples, becoming less and less human, more and more driving. Politics is no Great Disposer, no Divine Choice, no fatality of the gods, no mediaeval *Deus Vult*. It is a science, cold and calculating, not a utopian idealism. *Politics is history*. Economics sides with it, falls in tune, succeeds, triumphs, or goes bankrupt.

And here everything is measured to the city, where money has its home, its purpose, its message that reach out everywhere. For money is not only the supreme symbol; it is the real and *only* meaning of city life.

Today in the giant city—New York, London, Berlin, Moscow—history is made. In the countryside the peasant exists merely as a backdrop to history. It is cityscape *versus* landscape. It is the distinction that time has not altered nor history changed in the least, that deep-set difference—complete, absolute, irreconcilable—of a definite world-feeling. City intelligence, cold, mechanical, Natureless, is in direct opposition to the crafty, cunning, natural instinct of the peasant. For him life presents itself in relation to the land (Nature) permeated with timeless character; while for the City-man life is Natureless, artificially timewise. Intrinsically, it is a matter of money outlook (civism) as distinct from rural outlook (peasantry). Sunrise and sunset, planting-time and harvest-time, moon-phase and tidal-runs, earthquakes, floods, tempests—all these things for the true city dweller have no meaning whatever. Reality for him is always within the pavement world of flashing lights and deafening noises, of endless coming-and-going, pulsating (consciously or otherwise) to *money*; while the peasant, isolated, has long since turned his back to the city and has given his soul to the land. With its fashionable quarters, tourist centres and curiosities, its Jewish enclave, negro ghetto and slum areas, the giant city is a time-space world with its symbols and signs, its language and colour[1]—the like of which the peasant can never conceive, let alone understand.[2]

---

[1] The whole meaning of colour is brought immediately to mind at the mere thought of certain cities: Seville, Naples, Benares, let alone New York and London.

[2] The tacit difference is that of emphasis: the City-man sees the world as limited space, artificial, man-made; the peasant as endless earth and sky, timeless, eternal.

For the peasant the earth is eternal, for the City-man there is an arising, a beginning and—eventually—an end of that mass pile of edifices and houses we call a city. Some come and go (Imperial Rome), others suddenly vanish (Aztec Mexico). As in the past, so in the future, this or that city will rise with increasing sharpness—witness New York today—till it is complete. Then, bit by bit, it will crumple, disintegrate, or evolve into something else. How much does the Rome of Augustus, the Paris of Napoleon, tell us? And how much, in the highest sense of the word, does the peasant's landscape *not* tell us? Civilization endures as long as the city endures. When it dies, either by collapse or by cataclysm, life reverts to the countryside with its deposit of the eternal peasant.

Here is the supreme sign of the final hardening of our age: the city land wins out from the soil. The shop, the office, the factory outbid the farm. The neon-illuminated avenues, the noisy streets, the busyness of night-and-day life, appeal to the utopian dream of get-rich-quick. The increasingly numerous overpopulated cities result in the hall-mark of our age and time—the urbanization of mankind.

Time and Space have taken on undreamt-of proportions; science and the growth of cities have affected Western society with its emphasis on ease and security almost to a push-button convenience, not only anticipating, but already perfecting, the possibilities of atomic energy. But at what cost? The countryside is threatened to be overcome by the grasping tentacles of the giant city. Where yesterday stood a row of vacant houses, today stands a huge shopping centre and tomorrow whole areas transformed into cities-in-themselves, nothing more than expansions of the metropolitan area.[1] Future cities will encompass huge areas never even imagined, dooming the countryside to urban transformation or desolate waste.

Here, as always but with greater intensity, money plays a supreme role. For just as civilization is the dictatorial *power* of money in all its forms, so the city is the absolute *idea* of money, abstract and artificial, timeless and spaceless, extending to every known corner of the earth. For city thinking *par excellence* is in terms of money, of cash value, of profit and loss—*all abstractly*. But the farmer or peasant (it matters little what he is called) thinks not in figures, but in concrete goods, land, husbandry. It is, again, the eternal difference between Time and Space, between politics and religion, between the artificial world of the true city dweller and the sun-and-rain soaked earth of the peasant-farmer.

It is the style of a soul that comes out in the need for —or hatred of—city life. With its noise and filth, its daemonic energy, its chance for sudden fame and fortune, the city holds millions in her grasp, squeezes them dry and when no longer of any use finally lets them go—to die upon the pavement or to disappear in the open countryside.

[1] In Paris a whole new *arrondissement* has been designated to meet the problems of overpopulation.

CHAPTER FOUR

POLITICS SYNONYMOUS WITH DESTINY

FROM SUCH THINGS as the peasant alone can feel has arisen the makings of all religious movements. The more enigmatic and indefinable this feeling becomes—this knowing-without-being-able-to-explain—the more it possesses meaning. How much does the peasant accept, perform and take to his whole being with a profound mystical sense coupled with fear, because his will to understand it (intellect) is baffled. This time-space feeling of a religious stamp cannot be got rid of. It cannot be acquired by an outsider. Nor has it anything to do with the Bible which as world literature has no meaning (book value) for the peasant. Inherent in his whole being is a totally different world-outlook measured to the land (Nature), to reproduction, to plants and animals. Not only does this mystical land-religious attitude—staid, subaltern, peremptory—give him life, but it is Life itself, prone perhaps to change but never to direction. It is pristine and primordial, something he alone can understand, but cannot express, and in its presence the City-man for all his cleverness and intelligence remains non-plussed and dumb. It is the opposition of two completely different worlds. In Classical times it set apart the Roman centurion from the Aramean peasant. In our own it distinguishes the Milanese financier from the Sicilian fisherman, the New York executive from the Southern cotton picker. It is the pre-eminence of city intelligence—money and power—as opposed to earth, land, and sky.

Bitterly as we may feel the inner emptiness and poverty of religion, earnestly as we may long to be "religious," it is out of our power to do so. Religiousness, not religion, belongs to the giant city, to the educated megalopolitan, who lives mechanically rather than organically. It is synonymous with skyscrapers, factories, mass entertainment, and sports. In such a money-power setting, words like "God," "belief," "religion," "church," (which? and where?) sound empty, void of real meaning and significance.

No longer a part of the soil, man is a rootless animal hungry to opportunity in any cement-and-sidewalk periphery. No longer is "home" an idea, as well as an ideal, for which he is willing to fight and, if necessary, give up his life. Not a town or a province, or even a village or a hamlet, home is today a four-walled enclosure with its tempo of city life. Here and nowhere else does the lonely individual seek solace and refuge in nonentity, in that dry mediocrity of masswise, twentieth-century living. Struggle is an everyday necessity. From financiers to parasites, from big industrialists with their world empires to the hovels of beggars and thieves, it is an inevitable choice. And if man does not decide for himself, the forces of Nature will.

Today politics, race, and blood override religion, language, and intellect. The civilized man of the giant city, that object of worship and envy everywhere, alone counts and leaves a valid impression. Ever sceptical, practical, artificial, he lives consciously, lusting for power, money, possessions. His yearning spirit finds no resting place. He has no goal and no peace, and goes groping to the grave. He has altered little since the days of Juvenal. He still longs for two things: *panem et circenses.* Football and baseball, radio, cinema, television, newspapers and magazines—now replace the Circus Maximus. He either sees for himself (or has made seen for him) that *the* particular "religion" is the right one, and devoutly—"going to church"—acknowledges it. Or he turns aside, dabbles in something else, or merely avoids the whole issue.[1]

In the United States work is a religion, and pleasure a hard-centred indulgence. Success is synonymous with fat living and money getting. Vulgar diversions are a sordid escape from mechanical dryness—witness the need of toys, of games, of childish distractions. In a multi-racial society with its untenable faiths, reverence for deep spiritual things has become a form of lip service, a game, a sport, with all its gaiety and signficance.[2] There is nothing left to characterize a class but its money, which can be gained or lost overnight. Education is a prerequisite of obtaining better and more lucrative employment rather than a means of training the mind. Or as Plato saw it to produce courage in battle.

Modern man—the shifting mob living in an endless sea of houses—has become part of the rootless city mass. He is the avid newspaper-reader, the "educated" man of up-to-date magazines, novels, and best-sellers. He is the indispensable element of social events and cocktail

[1] Consider the Isis-cult in Republican Rome and the Isis-religion in Egypt. The one was a relaxation, a pastime, a fashion; the other, a deeply religious cult, an effective religion of the time. Likewise, consider Christian Science as a literary cliché of Christianity, and Christianity with its deep piety as the Puritans felt it and understood it.

[2] The United States, during its early growth and development, clung strongly to its puritan origins, to a very intense religious feeling, and to the submission to rules and the renunciation of oneself which according to Montesquieu was the very essence of Republican virtues. Albert Sorel, *Montesquieu*, p. 144.

D   [49]

parties, the ruck of amusement and sports, the snob, the literate, the aesthete, the wily politician and the retired general, who consider themselves entitled to rule. Politics is a game, a stepping-stone, a means of arriving, with lazy illusions of security, comfort, and well-being that only cash can buy.

Religion has always remained outside the biological make-up of man. True, it has awakened in him a great spiritual springtime and race-forming drive. It inspired the Crusades and the Moorish world of Spanish culture, the creation of Chartres and the flowering of Gothic art. It has given man belief in a world beyond the grave, has offered him inward peace and resignation before death, and has even provided a complete way of life.

But the ancient *vita contemplativa* no longer exists. Cash and not religion manifests itself, completely surpassing everything else. Money is an immense superiority, enjoying a power of every kind and in numberless forms. The soul may mutiny against it, but in the end is overcome.

Today we no longer know what deep religious feeling is. The incessant tempo of daily living, becoming more "modern," more speedy, more easily adaptable to the Anglo-American ideal of comfort and ease—lies alien to the world of deep religious thought.[1] No great personality, no saint, no new Jesus, Paul, Joachim of Floris, St. Francis has yet come forward to give a mystical-metaphysical form to this new (contemporary) world outlook. Man has become a slave to political, economic, social concepts rather than to a particular doctrine whereby he lives religiously, *from birth to death.* Imagine celibacy, poverty, pilgrimages—where?—self-mutilation,

---

[1] What is there in common between a Wall Street banker and a Franciscan monk, between a Parisian executive and a provincial curé, between a New York Society girl and a Sicilian nun?

and asceticism as practised in the seventeenth century—
in present-day New York, Chicago, London, or Berlin.
Scientific theories and technical achievements, the hall-
mark of our age, *lead away* from the priestly world. What
possible meaning could Einstein's Theory of Relativity
have, say, for a Neapolitan? Mathematical formulas
have nothing whatever to do with soul-belief any more
than mythology has with mysticism.

Today there is no religious ferment, no drive, no
springtime capable of inspiring and *creating* a whole
religious world of art. Synonymous with money and
power, Civilization, by its very definition, excludes religion with all its forms and expressions in terms of artistic
creation. Again, ours is not an age of Romanesque and
Gothic art, of such masterpieces as Vézelay and Chartres.
It is an age of the Machine. It is an atomic age with its
tactics and stratagems of war-preparedness taking final
shape in the background. The industrial, politico-
economic society of today has no place for the artist any
more than it has for the saint or poet. The artist exists
as a parasitic dilettante or as an out-and-out propagandist,
like Orozco, Rivera, and Picasso (*Guernica*). At best, he
is the man of our time, expressing the tragedy of war
and the pleasures of peace. But in a world that places
money above art, politics beyond religion, he is reduced
everywhere to a collector's level and to the filling-up of
museums, not so much in artistic value, if any, but in
cash. He remains outside society, an exception, not the
rule.[1]

[1] In the Classical world, art was created for the eye: the
Parthenon was for all to see and admire; whereas the music of Bach
is everywhere best understood by musicians. Art was conçeived of
as belonging to everyone and to a definite place: the acropolis, the
agora, the forum; whereas Hamlet, Don Quixote, Faust, Ivan
Karamazov, the "Mona Lisa," Michelangelo's "Night and Day"
belong to a room.

The profundity of a religion or the deep religious convictions of an inner life no longer triumph.[1] *They have ceased to be.* The age-old Christian outlook has been rejected, or has been cast aside as no longer feasible. Money has become, both in terms of cash and of imaginary values—power, wealth, possessions, social position— a god and the very meaning of life. Thinking confines itself more and more to science and, rightly enough in this atomic age, to technics. And technics, with their soulless attitude to man and life, are at once unfavourable to religion, art, and philosophy in the grand sense of the word.

The gigantic conflict between Papacy and Empire has come to a close. The purpose of the prevailing doctrine was perfectly clear, and its fateful legacy from the Gothic past was looked upon as the privilege of the learned, wealthy class—a privilege moreover that Marx and his successors achieved in shaking completely out of existence: something which only a century before would have been inconceivable, if not impossible. The aeroplane, the automobile, the skyscraper—these are the great signs and symbols, mechanical, soulless, of the age and world in which we live. These alone, for us, have meaning and purpose. The time for great art and philosophy is past, and our instinct for the realities of life tell us so. How meaningless are the pickings and stealings of modern art! Architecture, not paintings or sculpture, is the natural and *rightful* medium of capitalistic art-

---

[1] Witness the deep mystical, religious feeling that swept through the world in the days of Otto the Great (962). Or compare the Jewish assimilation and passiveness everywhere with the *spirit* of Jewry that swept over Palestine in 115 when Trajan marched into the East. A crusade of Jewry is no longer possible, since Jewishness, not Jewry as Josephus knew it and admired it, makes itself felt—a spirit, yes, but a diluted reflection of a long-forgotten inwardness.

expression. The skyscraper takes its place beside the Pyramids, the Colosseum, the Parthenon. The church, the cathedral, the stained-glass window, the statuary façade, belong to a religious past, to a historical yesterday that occupies Space and has a language in Time, but little else. Christian art is dead and buried and all pretence to express it in terms of religious art—*art sacré*—is merely a sham. Money and brains—political power, armies, wealth—these are the sister-symbols of our age of which the painter's voice is but a faint echo.

Today there is no idea of an awful End, of the Last Judgement, of Resurrection, Paradise and Hell; no conception of the earth's destiny and man's as One. No Messiah is awaited, with longing and desire. People live for today only, not for tomorrow. Living is horizontal, not vertical, and almost every high ideal in life has become largely, if not entirely, a question of *money*. Whether it is rightly earned, accepted, or even stolen, nobody cares. For money—by its very definition—is anything but sentimental. To be physically and spiritually and morally part of a great Culture with its traditions and its historical greatness, is hardly considered. Quality is replaced by quantity. Dignity of morals and manners, hauteur and elegance, taste and thought—let alone honour and bravery—all is pushed aside.

The United States, with its overlaying, its migrations, its adoptions, will soon undergo an inevitable blossoming: a ripening and transformation will take place. But only the forms and structures will change, not the climate or setting. An orientation, a direction, a goal of desire is set. Something—and this we cannot exactly foresee—is set for the future, probably in the first half of the next millenium—unless and until history decides otherwise.

Religion has given over—and rightly so—to politics.

Whereas Western man sees Christianity with its medi-aevalism, its puritanism, its anti-scientific outlook, more and more as a hindrance to his own life-feeling, Eastern man (Russian and Chinese) has long since embraced the State with an unconstrained, unfrustrated "logical" religion of his own. What is at stake for the whole world is not this or that religious creed, dogma, or belief but politics—high politics—which, rightly understood, is *synonymous with military destiny*.

Christianity is standing at a decisive point. Will it emerge victorious, or will it go down before Communism? It is established precedent that wants to continue, and recent Past that wants to be the Future. Each considers itself *the* future, although we who read these lines may not live to see the final (and fatal) outcome of the struggle. Hastened by atomic perfection, Christianity is moving relentlessly towards its logical conclusion. And the destiny of the Church is swept along with it. Christianity is trying to carry on a life that emerged long before the Aramaic seedtime; Communism is perfecting a doctrine that may achieve its goal—which is nothing less than world domination—as the other, tired, weary and worn, draws to a close.

CHAPTER FIVE

FORCES IN AN AGE OF CRISIS

THERE IS A new race of men who identify themselves not with genuine statesmanship but with politics, not with tradition but with money. Men of intellect without morals, ability without scruples, courage without honour, they seek after wealth and rank—*and obtain them*, and once in power render themselves capable of deeds and decisions to which otherwise they would never have risen. A party leader is always for himself as long as he has the Party behind him—Labour, Socialism, Communism, Democracy,[1] it makes no difference. In an economic world of capitalistic finance, trade unions, trusts and cartels, leaders, dictators, presidents, prophets and their adherents rise to the top by brains and fists, and maintain their position at any cost. For them the "people" is nothing but an object and all ideals merely means to an end. Similarly constitutions, treaties and schemes for world peace are (as always) merely pieces of paper. Newspapers, cash and the getting-of votes rule the masses. "Rights" and "liberties" fall in tune with the political forms of the moments. If the individual cannot be led, he will be *pushed* by a clever minority so that *their* purposes, not his, can be carried into effect.

"Democracy" and "progress" are part of the political catechism of our century, but for a handful of sceptics,

[1] Democracy of what? Who finances the press and the elections? Who gains by them?

such easy generalities ring with a hollow irony before the reality of poverty, famine, racial discrimination, nuclear annihilation. Our own century has been an era of tyranny, imperialism, and virtually constant warfare.

Democracy, far from being a political blessing, is a prime agent in the destruction of cultural values. A hundred per cent democracy is an impossibility: what naïve citizens call "democracy" is merely a halfway mark to a strong man's rise to power. Again, it is always a *minority* that rules and is *represented* in history. Political ideologies, Marxist or otherwise, are essentially meaningless: practical effectiveness alone counts. Force only—not words—"literature"—can decide. True political power means finance, capital and its agent, the press. The triumph of *money*—this, and nothing less, is the basis of political reality.

All dictatorship begins with an attempt to realize an ideal, but the ideal takes form, colour, meaning and direction from the persons who strive to realize it. Ideology degenerates into tyranny as soon as it establishes a dictatorship. We remember Robespierre, Hitler, and Stalin, but we forget Savonarola, Calvin, and John Knox. The fanatic, the ascetic, the priest always are the most dangerous kind of despot; fanatical terrorism is human nature at its worst; the strongest will is broken by the futility of the struggle.

Men rise to events to give distinction to their age— Luther, Frederick the Great, Goethe—and in our own Churchill, de Gaulle, Chou En-Lai. The statesman, the warrior, the saint, the thinker and the artist, only these does history remember, and rightly so. Today more than ever it is the sword and money that are influencing peoples everywhere. Ideas of freedom, justice, humanity, truth, progress—all go down before a leader's will-to-power. To repeat: it matters not so much what is the life-power of a party leader or of an officer-corps or even of whole armies as in China, but rather at whose *immediate disposal* it is. This, and nothing less, is the key to the secret of politico-military achievement. Again, politics is, and will be for many years, the fight for power in preparation for war. And here money plays its last great role. Men amass millions, not because they delight in wealth, let alone know how to use it, *but for power*. Besides, one can only make use of the masses when one has money, not before. For this reason democratic ethos is doomed before bigger and bigger money. Today the newspaper replaces the book. Nothing, for us, is so opposite as the dynamism of the press as Lord Beaverbrook understands it and the *Dialogues* of Plato. The one is Reality, the other—Truth. Books remain ever personal, but newspapers[1] with their far-reachingness shepherd the masses into the service of him who directs them. They order the thinking, direct the opinion (and consequently the action) of people everywhere. Constitutional rights mean nothing without money. How many elections are won before the first ballot is cast!

A society, state, or nation is vital only to the extent that it believes there are many things more important than the preservation of life.[2] Adventurers are no good in great moments of history; it is the sense of responsibility that is necessary, for without it disaster is inevitable.

Man, as a true leader, is out to *make* history. He wants to shape the world according to his own ideas, not become a nameless unit of any peasantry, army, or city mass.

---

[1] Including *Pravda* and the Red Army newspaper *Krasnaya Sviezda* (The Red Star).

[2] Machiavelli in his *Florentine History* maintains that the greatness of his native city was, in the first place, due to constant civil war and, in the second place, to the poverty of the inhabitants.

The politician and statesman want to rule, the *petit bourgeois* and merchant to trade and acquire wealth, the artist to create, the warrior to find glory in battle, the woman to bear children. And so man lives and dies, achieves eternal fame in the timewash of history or perishes, unremembered, in the anonymity of masswise existence—in that time-space stage which comprises the particular world selected by destiny to be his and no other. To the higher man life is not to be enjoyed, but achieved.

The maternal is inseparable from marriage—meaning children and race (ethos), not sentimental companionship. The real woman does not confuse man with motherhood but sees the logic that embraces her destiny : the child caressed by loving hands, and so succumbs to his will. The instinct for family, the desire to marry young and bear children—that is her role. She may deny it, but she can never alter it.

Intellectuals, literary promises and would-be poets[1] lie as always outside politics and therefore history. They may comment on it, reflect it, even in their own pitiful way express it, but make it—never. Literature is and remains—literature. Words have nothing whatever to do with blood. It is again, the unbridgeable gulf between truth and fact. Leaders hold their rank in respect to money, cash, power, never to books. Napoleon knew this, Marx and Rousseau, idealists *en grand*, not at all. Facts—and this must be incessantly repeated—are for the warrior, the statesman, who want to lead the people and fashion the world after their own ideas—or go down before history. Ideals are for the priest, the artist, the saint, who interpret the activity (History) of others. A

---

[1] Dante sacrificed the peace of his life to the ideal of *Una Italia*. Where are such poets today?

man who attempts to improve religion for political purposes is a fool. A sociologist-preacher who tries to bring
truth ("God"), righteousness, peace and forgiveness into
the world of actuality is a fool also.

Today more than ever it is a question of making
history or submitting to it. There is no place for
private wishes, romantic visions, personal whims. In the
collision of Fact with Truth force and mass will be more
decisive than matter and form. One thing is certain:
he who mobilizes the masses and controls the money and
forces *his* will on others will rule the world.

The great age of individualism is at hand. *It is the
clear Will-to-Power*. It is an age of Civilization, of
material forces, of money and power, not of Culture with
its spiritual awakening, its poetry, its art, and its religion.
It is a Roman age of dictatorship which shoves aside
completely the tendency to dream of world peace, of
happiness "forever and ever." To make the world their
own, not to preserve the principles and ideals of a decaying civilization, is the destiny of a select few who,
like Alexander, Caesar, and Napoleon, will force their
will on others to write the next great chapter in
history.

In a democracy-world money has won out over intelligence, hard cash over intellect. Respect is only for
power, money, wealth. The political "beat" and life
style is that of force-men in unrestrained competition for
supreme power—nothing less will suffice. When democracy loses its hand, force and violence come into their
own; cash and power (moneyed might), not tradition
and authority, win out in the end.

The masses, unchanged since Caesar's time, live a
hand-to-mouth existence. Yet it is only a step from
misery to rebellion, from street-fighting to open revolution. Stirred to fury, the masses can rise in revolt.

Beaten and terrorized the negro—not only in the United States but above all in Africa—yearns for liberty, and is willing to pay with his life for a chance to achieve it. Mob-rule will give way to a leaderless power, freedom will bow to sordid financial interests, and democracy will go down in ruin before—Communism.

Life is a process, then, of affecting immediate possibilities. More than ever, it is the organic and humanly irreducible opposition of the world of ideas and the world of material forces, that deadly enmity of Money and Intellect as *separate ideals*, inwardly and not merely nominally. It is also a courageous fatalism before the great reality of facts, in face of which all theological writing is irrelevant and all political "theories" futile.

The heyday of Anglo-American imperialism and the aureole of its unchallenged prestige, is no longer. The fall of the European *imperium* in Asia and the Middle East destroyed a once-powerful and effective political framework which gave security, domestic order, and prosperity to many countries. Ours, again, is an age of out-and-out effort and (in mechanistic terms) of man *as instrument*. It stands as a half-way mark between the ancient totalitarianism of Church and Empire, and the new totalitarianism of this, the Marxist-spreading, Communist-inspired modern world.

What if, one day, politicians and the underworld join forces to make an end of the existing order? What if some Catlinarian adventurer, inspired by Communist promises of power and glory, should suddenly throw caution to the winds and tempt fate with open revolution? A class war, dictated by Moscow (past masters in the art of intrigue, bribery, and the power of gold) could outdo the Parisian horrors of 1792. History awaits the man who has everything to gain and nothing to lose—except his life. And the danger has at no time been greater than in these years.

To confuse reality with a wish-picture of the future is disaster. In the coming struggle all is at stake. Courage is never enough, for without the will-to-victory it is useless. Intelligence, standing up to danger, readiness for great sacrifices—only these qualities can save a nation from going under.

The future in every age belongs to those who see further than others and who fight their way upwards towards the rightful goal that is theirs. *Fortune smiles only on the bold.* But great deeds are not accomplished without major risks and self-sacrifice. That is the all-powerfulness of success and the pride, such as the great Romans knew, of world achievement. It is the supreme *homage* that our age can pay to any man.